GOLFER'S LITTLE
BOOK OF WISDOM

by
Sean Doolin

ICS BOOKS, Inc.
Merrillville, IN

Golfer's Little Book of Wisdom

Copyright © 1997 by Sean Doolin   Cover photo: Warren Morgan / H. Armstrong Roberts

10 9 8 7 6 5 4 3 2 1

All inquiries should be addressed to ICS Books, Inc., 1370 E. 86th Place, Merrillville, IN 46410

Published by:	**Co-Published in Canada by;**	**Printed in the U.S.A.**
ICS BOOKS, Inc.	Vanwell Publishing LTD	
1370 E. 86th Place	1 Northrup Crescent	
Merrillville, IN 46410	St. Catharines, Ontario	
800-541-7323	L2M 6P5	
	800-661-6136	

Library of Congress Cataloging-in-Publication Data

Doolin, Sean.
      Golfer's little book of wisdom / by Sean Doolin.
      p.   cm. -- (Little book of wisdom series)
      ISBN 1-57034-063-3 (pb)
1. Golf.
                              I. Title. II Series .
                              GV965.D64 1997
                              796.352--dc21   96-29840
                                                                           CIP

Preface

Everyone and their brother is playing golf these days; wouldn't it be nice if they actually knew what they were doing? Here are some hints and tips for the novice and even the seasoned golfer. Easy, concise and simple methods to help you get that little white ball in the hole without using higher math to figure out your score when it's over. This book is designed to give basic techniques and proper etiquette so people taking up the game will enjoy themselves and won't hold up the entire course. Just one tip could shave strokes off your game.

1.   Standing tall during a bunker shot helps avoid touching the sand with the club.

2.   When paired up with a stranger always introduce yourself before you tee off.

3. Write down the person's name you get paired up with on your scorecard so you don't forget it.

4. Exercise will improve your mobility and stamina.

5. Clean your ball before you tee off on each hole.

6. Proper stance dictates bending at the hip joint not at the waist.

7.   A draw is a shot that tails off to the left
     (right handed shot) at the end of the
     ball's trajectory.

8.   A fade is a shot that tails off to the right
     (right handed shot) at the end of the
     ball's trajectory.

9. Your knees should be slightly bent during your swing.

10. Your weight should be distributed evenly.

11. Remember that yardage markers are measured from the middle of the green out.

12. Watching your shadow during practice
     swings allows for live critiquing of your
     swing.

13. A bunker and a sand trap are the same
     thing.

14. Carrying several clubs to a blind shot can speed up one's round.

15. Volunteering to work a professional tournament is a great way to meet your heros.

16.   A birdie is one shot under par.

17.   An eagle is two shots under par. Three
       shots under would be a double eagle.

18. Make sure your clubs are dry before putting them away. Rust is cancer to a golf club.

19. To open your club face you must turn your club slightly clockwise (right handed shot) and swing normally.

20.	Opening the club face during a bunker shot allows the club to move through the sand easily.

21.	A chip shot is any shot within 5 paces of the green.

22. A slice is a shot that drastically curves to the right of your target (right handed shot) due to the clockwise spin on the ball.

23.   To make your shot slice, just play your
      front foot forward a couple of inches
      from your normal stance and swing
      normally.

24. Put a set amount of money into a "Golf get-a-way fund" every time you get a birdie or better.

25. A pitch shot is any shot 5 paces or more away from the green up to 100 yards.

26. A hook is a shot that drastically curves to the left of your target (right handed shot) due to the counterclockwise spin on the ball.

27.   To make your shot hook, just drop your
      front foot a couple of inches behind
      your normal stance and swing normally.

28.   Always promote fast play.

29.   Keep your ball in your pocket on cold days before you tee off.

30.   Total your score at the next tee, not on the green.

31. Pete Dye used to sell insurance - yet another reason to dislike him.

32. To close the club face you must turn the club counter clockwise (right handed shot) slightly and swing normally.

33.   If your ball's path starts out and
        continues right, try closing the club
        face.

34.   Have your eyes examined yearly.

35.   You can't play well if you can't see
        well.

36. A bogey is one shot over par. Two shots over par would be a double bogey then triple bogey and so on.

37. You are only allowed 14 clubs in your bag at one time.

38. In a bunker, imagine a divot the size of a dollar with the ball directly in the center of the dollar.

39. Always take a full swing while hitting a bunker shot.

40. As your ball lands mark the area by
     remembering a tree, bush or fence
     nearby.

41.   After hitting the ball badly, realize what
       you did wrong, correct the problem,
       and don't get angry.

42. If there isn't anybody in front of you, it is always a good idea to let faster golfers play through.

43.   Replacing your divot only takes a few
seconds yet improves the condition of
the course immensely.

44.   Know the hole before you play it.

45.   Check for traps and water ahead before you tee off.

46.   Keeping your feet shoulder width apart during a drive allows for good balance during the swing.

47. Pointing your toes slightly outward during a drive allows for a fuller swing.

48. Knowing how far you hit a 6 iron is more important than how far someone else hits a 6 iron.

49. Anyone who refuses to practice on the range also refuses to improve their game.

50. Keep some sun block in your bag to protect your face and ears.

51. Play a championship course to see how you compare with the pros.

52. Enjoy the scenery.

53. Caffeine and sugar are not going to help you relax your stance.

54.   A lost ball is a 2 stroke penalty.

55.   Golf Law #286 - The smaller the tree in your path, the greater your chance of hitting it.

56.   Plant your feet deep in a bunker for a more stable swing.

57. Always clean your golf spikes before you leave the course.

58. Never talk during someone else's swing.

59. Imagine the path of a pendulum during
     your back swing and the follow
     through.

60. Your grip should be tight enough to hold an egg but not tight enough to crush it.

61. Practice putting on a flat part of a green to get a feel for a standard stroke.

62. Imagine the desired path of the ball before hitting the ball.

63.   Practice chipping at the park.

64.   Practice sand shots at the beach.

65.   Concentrate on your game, not on your score.

66.   Practice your putting.

67.   The green represents half of your score.

68.   Get off the course immediately at the first "crack" of lightning.

69. Lightning can strike 5 miles before the storm front.

70. Don't play the same brand ball as someone else in your foursome.

71. Always pass along proper golf etiquette to misinformed partners.

72. Keep your head down until the momentum of your arms and shoulders carries through bringing your head up with them.

73. Keeping your arms and neck tense during your swing can lead to injury.

74. Always yell, "Fore!" if you accidentally hit your ball at someone else.

75. Always look to see where the pin is placed before hitting to the green.

76. Putting tape on the face of your club on the practice tee shows you where the ball is hitting your club face.

77. Taping your name, address, and phone number near the grip of your clubs can lead to fewer lost clubs.

78.   A well padded shoulder strap can save
       you a lot of pain and suffering on the
       course.

79.   Always cover the back of your head near the spine when someone yells "Fore!"

80. Having an extra ball in your pocket can speed up your game after losing your ball.

81. Golf Law #149 - The louder your golf pants, the easier it is for someone to spot you cheating.

82. A downhill left breaking putt is the toughest putt in golf.

83. Keep a towel in/on your bag in case your grips get wet.

84. Put your wallet, keys and jewelry in your golf bag.

85. Standing up straight using only your arms (locked wrists) on a chip shot will improve your aim as well as feel for distance on the shot.

86. Never bet with someone whose ball is already in the hole.

87.   Beginners belong on a driving range
      before they get on the golf course
      (unless the course is empty).

88.   On hot days wear light colored clothing.
      On colder days wear darker clothing.

89. Your target should be in a line parallel to an imaginary line drawn from toe to toe. A club on the ground can help to visualize this line.

90. Save your old clubs for someone taking up the game.

91. Wear a hat while on the course. Skin cancer is a very serious problem for golfers.

92. There is no such thing as a foot wedge. That is a 1 stroke penalty.

93.   Always return items found on the course to the clubhouse lost and found.

94.   If you discover that you have lost something on the course go to the clubhouse lost and found the next time you are there.

95. Holding a towel under your upper left arm during your swing can help cure a slice.

96. Your hips will directly face the target at the completion of your swing.

97.　Balance is the key to a good golf shot.
　　　Try not to sway during your swing.

98.　If your spouse plays golf you'll always
　　　have someone to golf with on vacation.

99. Always get to the course before your tee time.

100. The worse you are at golf the more exercise you get on the course.

101. Find out if someone wants suggestions before giving them. Nobody likes a know-it-all.

102. Remember that golf is a "game" that is to be enjoyed even if your not particularly good at it.

103. Even Greg Norman shoots an
     occasional quadruple bogey.

104. Playing golf once a week keeps your
     game regular.

105. Playing more than once a week helps you improve.

106. Driving is for show and putting is for the dough.

107. Keep a golf glove in your bag in case it rains and your grips get wet.

108. Golf takes days to learn and a lifetime to master.

109. Let the group ahead of you hit their second shot before you tee off.

110. The harder you try to kill the ball the less likely you are to hit it well.

111. Walking 18 holes is great exercise.

112. Try to keep some bug repellent in your bag at all times.

113. If you allow yourself to cheat you will never be able to improve.

114. Keep 1 opposite handed club in your
bag for obstructed shots.

115. Don't put your car keys in your golf
cart. You'll never find them later.

116. Remember that the group ahead of you is teeing off while you are on the green. Try to keep cheers and celebrations to yourself.

117. If an opposite handed club is not available, try pointing the toe of the club toward the ground and swinging opposite handed.

118. Take care of your clubs and they will take care of you.

119. Walk off yardage to your ball from yardage markers.

120. Red yardage markers are 100 yards out
from the middle of the green.

121. White yardage markers are 150 yards
out from the middle of the green.

122. Blue yardage markers are 200 yards out from the middle of the green.

123. Some courses mark the yardage to the middle of the green on the sprinkler heads in the fairway.

124. Golf balls make great inexpensive gifts for friends who play.

125. Coupon clipping is a great way to save money on golfing.

126. Try using a 7 or 8 iron on short chip shots with a lot of green between you and the cup.

127. If you miss your putt pay attention to the break before and/or after the hole so it only takes one more stroke to get it in.

128. Keep the flag from flapping in the wind while tending the pin.

129. Never leave a "birdie" putt short.

130. Don't try teaching someone how to play golf unless you and they have a lot of patience.

131. 75% of all golfers don't break 100 per round.

132. Never assume your clubs will get special handling. Pack them in a hard carrying case for airplane travel.

133. Replace the covers on your clubs after every shot so the clubs don't get nicked or scratched.

134. There is no such thing as a Mulligan. If you take one you are cheating.

135. Always be aware of other golfers on the course.

136. A typical round of golf should only take 3-4 hours.

137. Keep your golf cart on cart paths at all times.

138. Repairing your ball mark on the green only takes 20 seconds.

139. Repaired ball marks on the green heal in 1-2 days.

140. Non-repaired ball marks on the green take 2 weeks or more to heal.

141. Always call and cancel your tee time if you will not be able to make it.

142. Use a coin to mark your ball on the green so it is not in someone's line to the hole.

143. You can not pick up your ball for any reason until it is on the green.

144. The golf course is a beautiful place, please remember to keep it that way.

145. Every time you touch the sand with your club in a bunker it is 1 stroke. Even if you are just practice swinging.

146. You must play the ball as it lies.

147. You may not remove any natural obstructions in order to make a shot.

148. Keep your eye on your partner's ball. He is keeping his head down and may lose sight of it.

149. Always stretch and warm up before you start your round.

150. Colored balls can be difficult to spot during the fall season.

151. Always make a point to apologize if you almost hit another group with your ball.

152. Always rake your trap after a sand shot.

153. Try golfing with people you know are better than you. Their habits and game strategies can rub off on you.

154. Never intentionally hit up on the group in front of you to speed them up.

155. Always look around the green for clubs. Going back to get them later holds up the rest of the course.

156. Never loan your clubs out.

157. Don't use profanity on the course. It won't improve the way you play.

158. Always take water or some other beverage with you on the course.

159. Make sure you have enough tees and balls to finish your round before you tee off.

160. Making a tee time before you arrive at the course can save you a great deal of time.

161. Always call the course ahead of time to see if they have leagues or outings on the course.

162. Always ask to try out a new set of clubs before purchasing it.

163. Greens tend to break in the direction of natural bodies of water nearby.

164. Greens tend to be slower in the afternoon since the grass has had time to grow.

165.   Make sure you tee your ball up on level
       ground.

166.   It is a good idea to take an umbrella
       along with you golfing.

167.   You may not tee off in front of the tee
       markers.

168. Use the name printed on the ball to line up your putt.

169. Imagine a spot about 2 feet in front of your ball to help concentrate on the preferred line for your putt.

170. You may tee off up to one club length behind the tee markers.

171. Never try to hit your ball out of an area marked "under repair." You are allowed a free drop.

172. Wear loose clothing when golfing to allow for a full range of motion.

173. Always check for important items in your cart before you leave the course.

174. Never bet more than you can afford to lose.

175. A video camera is a great way to find flaws in your swing.

176. Try to plan an annual family golf outing. It will get easier and more fun each year.

177. Make sure your passenger is completely in the cart before taking off.

178. Always check the fuel or power gauge before leaving the clubhouse with your cart.

179. The person with the lowest score on the previous hole has the honor of teeing off first.

180. Your head should be behind the ball before you start your back swing.

181. You must pull the flag out of the cup
     when your ball is on the green before
     putting.

182. Don't stand in others' line of view
     while they are shooting.

183. Hit a ball laterally out of a trouble spot into the fairway rather than through the trouble toward the hole.

184. Always hit through the ball.

185. The golfer is usually responsible for any damage or injury caused by his/her golf ball.

186. Practice with 1 club on the range until you have mastered it before moving on to another club.

187. Your back swing should have the same speed and tempo as your swing and follow through.

188. On an uphill lie play the ball toward your forward foot.

189. Know your handicap so you can be paired up with equal players in outings and tournaments.

190. The ball should sit 3/4 of the way up the club face while on the tee.

191. Oversized clubs do not give more distance but they do have a bigger sweet spot allowing for a greater margin of error.

192. Keep your body stiff and your wrists loose during a bunker shot.

193. When chipping to the green you can expect the ball to fly 1/3 of the way and roll 2/3 of the way to the hole.

194. Learn the rules of the game before you get out on the course.

195. Always keep some extra money in your bag.

196. "Gimmies" are allowed however, they must be offered by another golfer in your foursome.

197. The back swing on a chip shot shouldn't go back past the knee.

198. Practice your swing in your garage or basement all year round.

199. Make sure the ceiling is high enough first.

200. The ball should be placed just inside the front foot when teeing off.

201. Stand closer to the ball for a chip shot.

202. Backspin is created by the club pushing the ball down into the ground and taking a divot.

203. On an uphill lie make sure your
shoulders are parallel with the slope of
the hill.

204. Helping a person in your foursome find his/her ball can speed up your round.

205. Refueling at the half way house helps keep your strength up for the rest of the round.

206. Every time the club touches the ball is 1 stroke no matter how far the ball goes or doesn't go.

207. A shot that can't be made in your mind can not be made on the course either.

208. Practice putting on your carpet in your house all year round.

209. Indoor golf businesses are popping up
all over the country. This is a good way
to keep in practice during the winter
months.

210. Make sure the club face is aiming
directly at your target before you set up
in your stance.

211. Take your clubs with you at all times. You never know when the opportunity to play will arise.

212. On a side hill lie with your feet above the ball, aim to the left of your target. The ball will naturally travel to the right.

213. Save the drinking of alcohol until the 19th hole.

214. It doesn't matter how big you are. Tiger Woods can hit the ball as far as John Daly.

215. Always remember to replace the flag back into the hole when finished.

216. Always take a club with you into the brush when looking for your ball. Alligators and snakes have no respect for the game.

217. The grips on your clubs should be tacky to the touch.

218. Have your clubs re-gripped by someone who knows what they are doing.

219. Keep your head down until your back shoulder touches your chin during your follow through.

220. Remember to park your cart far enough away from your ball so that you have an unobstructed shot.

221. Don't borrow clubs unless you are willing and able to pay for lost or damaged clubs.

222. On a side hill lie with your feet below the ball aim to the right of your target. The ball will naturally go to the left.

223. On a downhill lie play the ball closer to your back foot.

224. On a downhill lie make sure your shoulders are parallel with the slope of the hill.

225. On a side hill shot with ball above your feet choke down on your club.

226. When driving into heavy wind choke down on the club and close your stance.

227. When driving into heavy wind make
      sure the ball is either centered or closer
      to your front foot.

228. If the distance you want is between
      clubs, take the lower iron and swing
      lighter.

229. You should be trying to hit the ball on the bottom near the ground with the club face.

230. For a shot with less loft try gripping the club at the bottom of the grip.

231. Use this less loft technique for hitting shots directly into strong winds.

232. For a shot with more loft try gripping the club at the top of the grip.

233. Use this high loft technique to drive over trees in your ball's path.

234. Always let someone in your foursome know if you have allergies. Especially if you're allergic to bee stings.

235. If the sand is wet and firm or dry and fluffy play your bunker shot the same way.

236. When faced with a deep rough shot try putting more weight on your front foot and punching the ball out.

237. Your whole body should be still when putting, using your arms and shoulders only for a smooth stroke.

238. Use the practice green to practice your stroke not to test green speeds.

239. Course greens will probably play
     differently than the practice greens.

240. Take a practice swing to make sure you
     will hit the ball and not the ground.

241. If your practice swing was bad then you will probably hit the ball badly.

242. When putting, try to notice if the grain of the green is coming toward you or going away.

243.   Putts going with the grain will be faster.

244.   Putts going against the grain will tend
        to be slower.

245. The faster the ball travels on a putt the
less break it will have on the green.

246. The slower the ball travels on a putt the
more the break.

247. If you're having trouble lining up your putts, try switching your hands around on the putter.

248. Graphite shafts are considerably lighter than steel shafts.

249. You get a free drop from any man made obstacle like sprinkler heads or cart paths.

250. You should slow your swing down when using Graphite clubs.

251. Most courses have some natural marker (commonly an evergreen tree) to mark 150 yards to the green.

252. Steel shafts allow more touch and the ability to shape shots.

253. A graphite shaft club is more forgiving.

254. A steel shaft club is more precise.

255. Always clean the debris from the path of your putt before you putt.

256. Wet greens play slower and with less break than they would if they were dry.

257. Concentrate on keeping your back leg slightly bent throughout your swing for more power.

258. Always check the direction and speed of the wind before your shot. The wind will have a dramatic effect on the accuracy of the shot.

259. Use a lower club when hitting out of the rough, as longer grass will take some power away from your club.

260. When putting into the wind widen your stance and choke down a little on the club.

261. Strong winds will also affect your putts. Consider this before marking your line.

262. Never bet with anyone who has a 1 iron in his/her bag.

263. Never use a wood when hitting out of the rough.

264. Always bring rain gear in your bag.

265. Cover your clubs with your umbrella so the grips don't get wet.

266. It is a good idea to attach your club covers to your bag.

267. Always bring a divot repair tool with you.

268. You can fix other people's divots while you wait.

269. If you don't have a divot repair tool, try using a golf tee instead.

270. Always carry an extra pencil in your bag.

271. Keep track of how many putts it takes you to get the ball into the hole.

272. You should average 2 or less putts per hole per round.

273. If you are averaging more than 2 putts per hole this is the part of your game that should receive your undivided attention.

274. Always cross the fairway at a 90 degree angle in your golf cart.

275. Keep an extra score card in your bag.

276. When practicing give yourself a bad lie.
Chances are this is the shot you will
have on the course.

277. You get a free drop out of standing water on the green or in a bunker but no closer to the hole.

278. Schedule enough time to finish your round. It does you no good to hurry every shot.

279. Always count your clubs before and after your round.

280. The longer the club shaft, the more distance you will get on your shot.

281. The longer the club shaft, the greater the margin of error on hitting the sweet spot of the club.

282. Make sure you pick up your feet on the green while wearing golf spikes.

283. Wearing sunglasses is alright but take them off to putt. You won't be able to see the grain or breaks on the green with them on.

284. Don't spend more than 5 minutes looking for your ball.

285. Don't go hunting around all of the water hazards for balls.

286. Practice the shots that are difficult for you, not the ones that you consistently make well.

287. Try to play from the pro tees sometimes and see how hard they have it.

288. Instructional videos are an excellent addition to normal practice.

289. Most people worry about how to put
     backspin on the ball when they
     typically hit the ball short of the hole in
     the first place. If you aren't hitting the
     ball past the hole then why do you need
     backspin?

290. Respect the people who take care of the course. The harder they work, the more you enjoy the game.

291. Concentrate on your follow through during your swing.

292. Spend time practicing 2, 3 and 4 foot putts. These will drive you crazy if you miss them on he course.

293. The more routine a short putt is for you the less pressure is felt on par and birdie putts.

294. Buy golf equipment at the end of the golf season. Most pro shops have great deals then.

295. Never try to "soup up" your golf cart. They have governors on them for a reason.

296. Golf carts do not have seat belts so don't try taking turns at high speeds.

297. Don't stand behind someone when they swing.

298. Club heads have been known to fly off of the shaft.

299. Never pick up a ball that you know is not your own.

300. Put a mark on your ball so you can identify it.

301. Golf leagues are a great way to motivate you to play at least once a week. Join with a friend.

302. Keep a small first aid kit in your golf bag.

303. Recommend this book to a friend who would like to shave a few strokes off their scorecard.